Creative Brazilian
DRUMMER

BY CHRISTIANO GALVÃO

Edited by Rick Mattingly

Photo by Paulo Marconi

ISBN 978-1-4234-7770-9

HAL•LEONARD®
CORPORATION
7777 W. BLUEMOUND RD. P.O. BOX 13819 MILWAUKEE, WI 53213

In Australia Contact:
Hal Leonard Australia Pty. Ltd.
4 Lentara Court
Cheltenham, Victoria, 3192 Australia
Email: ausadmin@halleonard.com.au

Visit Hal Leonard Online at
www.halleonard.com

CONTENTS

ABOUT THE AUTHOR

Christiano Galvão was born in 1971 in Brazil. He is one of the most in-demand drummers in Rio de Janeiro.

He started his career as a self-taught drummer at the age of 13. Later, he took private lessons with great drum teachers such as Ronaldo Alvarenga, Damaso Cerruti, Pascoal Meireles and Márcio Bahia. In 1988 he studied at the Brazilian Music Conservatory (RJ).

In the early 1990s at age 19 he got his first major gig with the band of blues guitarist Celso Blues Boy. He toured with the group for almost three years, recording his first professional record, the live album *Celso Blues Boy Live* (1992).

In 1994 he moved to New York City to study at the renowned drum school Drummers Collective. He took lessons from Chip Fabrizi, Sandy Gennaro, Bobby Sanabria, and Fred Klats, and attended workshops with Simon Phillips, Dave Weckl, Steve Smith, and Omar Hakim.

After returning to Brazil in 1995 he started to play with several local artists. By the end of 1999 he was invited to join the band of singer/composer Zélia Duncan. It was a four-year association, during which he toured all over the country and in Portugal. He recorded Duncan's acclaimed CD/DVD *Sortimento Live* (2002).

Another long partnership was with singer/composer Jorge Vercillo. This lasted for over ten years and included touring all over Brazil with huge success. Christiano recorded four albums with Vercillo including the platinum *Elo* (2002) and two DVDs.

Since then Christiano has played and recorded with such great Brazilian artists as Simone, Marina Lima, Jorge Ben Jor, Jorge Aragão, Beth Carvalho, Isabella Taviani, Lenine, Rosa Maria Colyn, Belchior, and Daniel Gonzaga, among others.

In 2006 he released his first solo CD, *1+1*, made in partnership with bassist Alexandre Cavallo. The album received good reviews.

At present he is on tour with singer Simone and performing shows and running workshops based on his solo album. He also writes instructional articles for the Brazilian drum magazine *Modern Drummer Brasil*.

Christiano endorses Vic Firth sticks, Zildjian cymbals and Gretsch drums.

Visit his website at www.christianogalvao.com

INTRODUCTION

Creative Brazilian Drumming is a drum guide that will teach you exercises and grooves based on such Brazilian rhythms as baião, samba, maracatu, and frevo. The purpose of this book is not only to present the traditional Brazilian rhythms but also to share my personal approach to them, giving you tools that will stimulate your creativity on the drums.

This book includes a CD that contains all the musical examples, five complete tunes, and play-along tracks. In each song you will hear a two-measure count-off.

The chapters begin with a basic rhythm followed by the exercises and some groove applications. At the end of each chapter, you will find a drum chart that you can use to play along with the CD. You can also choose a slow or a fast tempo version of the tunes (see CD track index). At this point you will have a chance to apply the studied material, practicing your chart reading as well.

To get more into Brazilian culture, I recommend that you listen to recordings to learn how Brazilian songs are traditionally structured and played and where they came from. At the end of this book I listed a few titles that will help you to start your fascinating voyage into Brazilian rhythms.

Consider this book as a practical guide of ideas and grooves that you can use to enrich your musical vocabulary.

Have fun!
Christiano Galvão

KEY

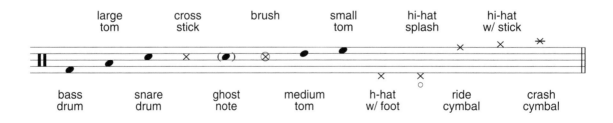

CHAPTER 1
BAIÃO
Foot Coordination

The following foot exercises are based on a rhythm from the northeast of Brazil called baião. Once you have mastered different foot ostinatos, you will be able to play and create interesting grooves. Look at the foot ostinato on this basic baião example. Notice that the left foot is playing upbeats:

TRACK 1

BAIÃO

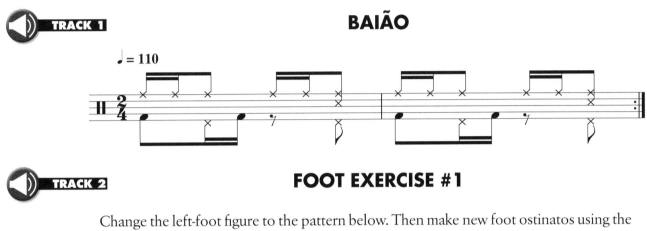

TRACK 2

FOOT EXERCISE #1

Change the left-foot figure to the pattern below. Then make new foot ostinatos using the bass drum patterns.

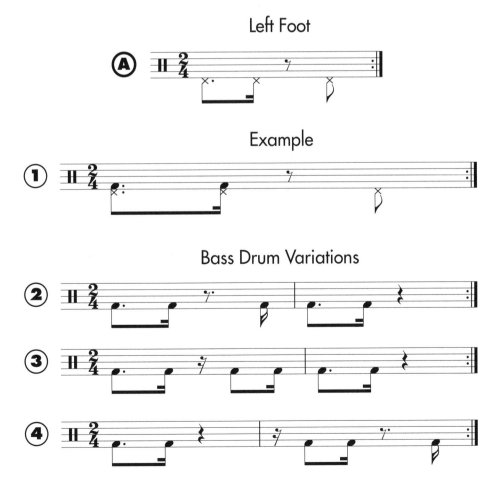

OSTINATO #1
w/ Bass Drum variations

Play the bass drum patterns over the following ostinato (B):

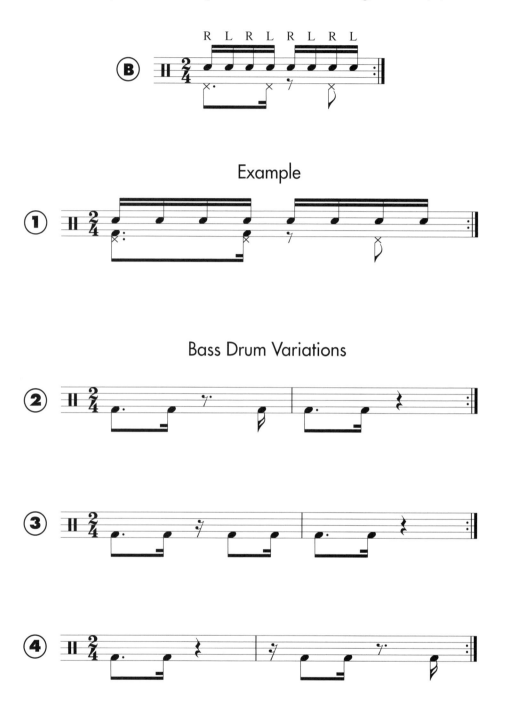

Example

Bass Drum Variations

Play exercises 1 through 4 at a fast tempo. Repeat each pattern twice.

2

 **TRACK 4**

FOOT EXERCISE #2

Play a basic baião bass drum figure with the right foot (C). Then make foot ostinatos by adding the following left-foot patterns:

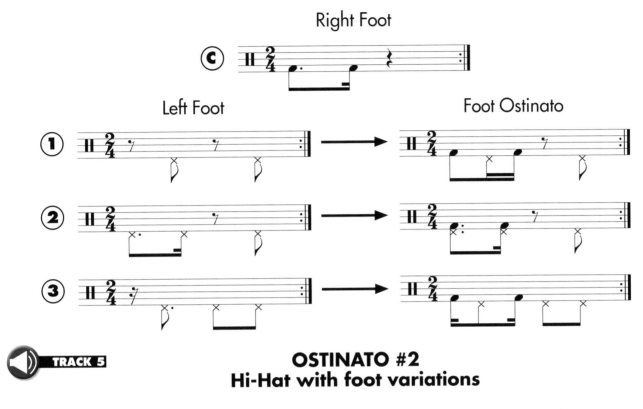

 **TRACK 5**

OSTINATO #2
Hi-Hat with foot variations

Play the hi-hat with foot patterns over the following baião ostinato (D).

P R A C T I C E   P R O C E D U R E

Play exercises 1, 2, and 3 nonstop at a fast tempo. Play eight times each.

GROOVES

The following grooves show some ways to use the foot variations patterns.

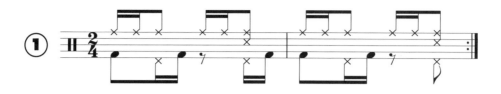

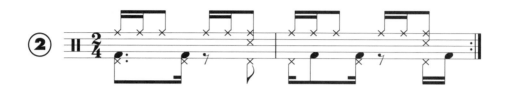

BAIÃO SOLO

Play a solo over this baião foot ostinato.

This page has been left blank to facilitate page turns for chart reading practice.

Baião Chart

"Pumpkin with Coconut"

Alexandre Cavallo/Christiano Galvão

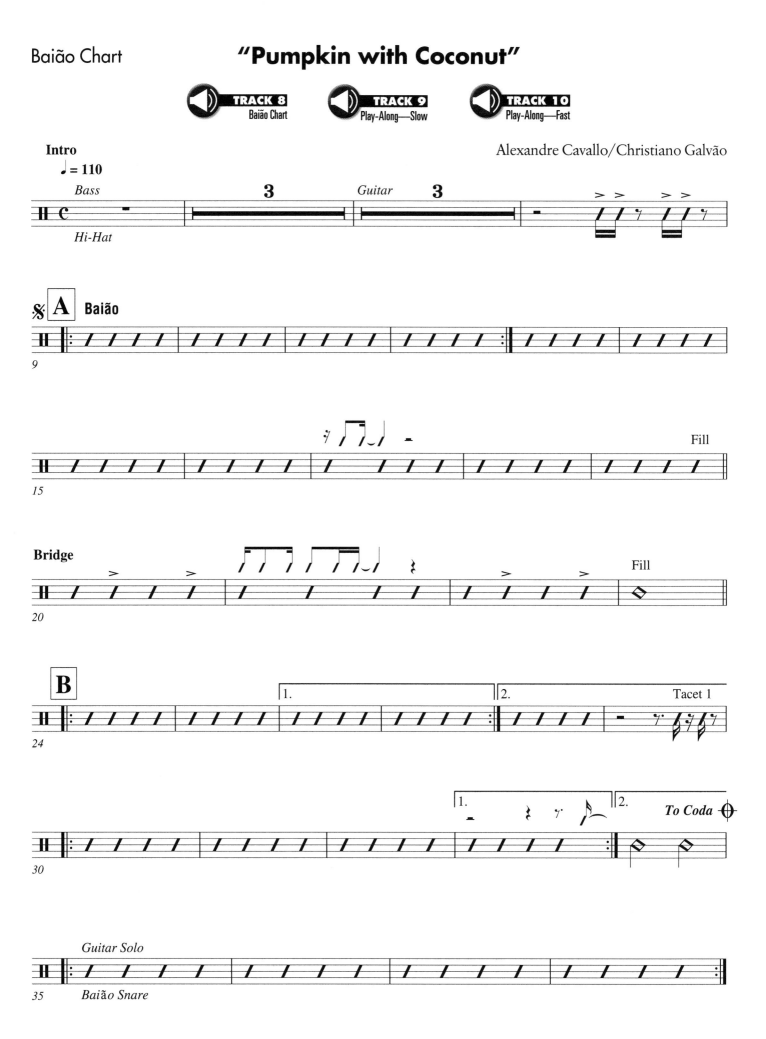

CHAPTER 2
MARACATU
Hand and Foot Independence

Practice hand and foot independence playing the great Brazilian rhythm called maracatu.

MARACATU

Notice that the buzz stroke is only on the snare drum.

MARACATU PATTERNS

The following patterns come from Cassio Cunha. Play the maracatu patterns separately, one each time. Notice that each one has a corresponding number that will be used in the following exercises.

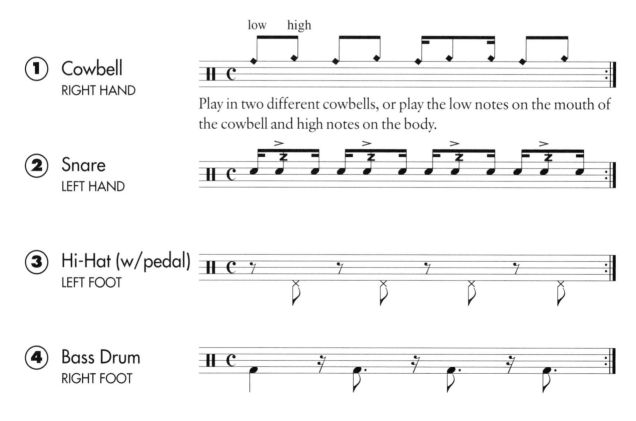

① Cowbell RIGHT HAND

Play in two different cowbells, or play the low notes on the mouth of the cowbell and high notes on the body.

② Snare LEFT HAND

③ Hi-Hat (w/pedal) LEFT FOOT

④ Bass Drum RIGHT FOOT

INDEPENDENCE EXERCISE #1

Use the following sequence (A–H) to play the maracatu patterns. Start with pattern 1 (cowbell). Play the entire exercise nonstop from the first to the last example. (The numbers refer to the previous patterns.)

PATTERNS

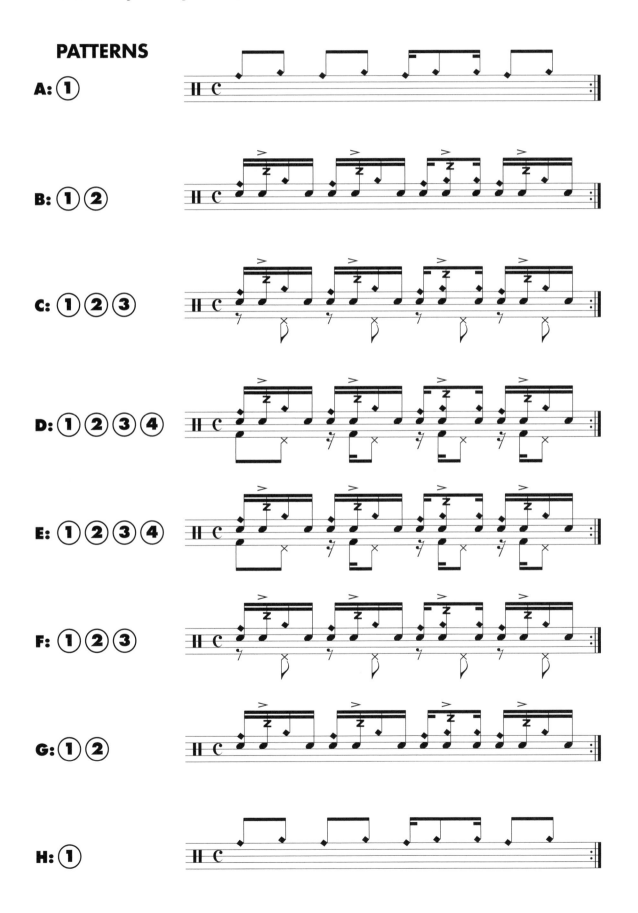

 **TRACK 14**

INDEPENDENCE EXERCISE #2

Use the following sequence (A–H) to play the maracatu patterns. Start with pattern 4 (bass drum). Play the entire exercise nonstop from the first to the last example. (The numbers refer to the patterns on page 8.)

PATTERNS

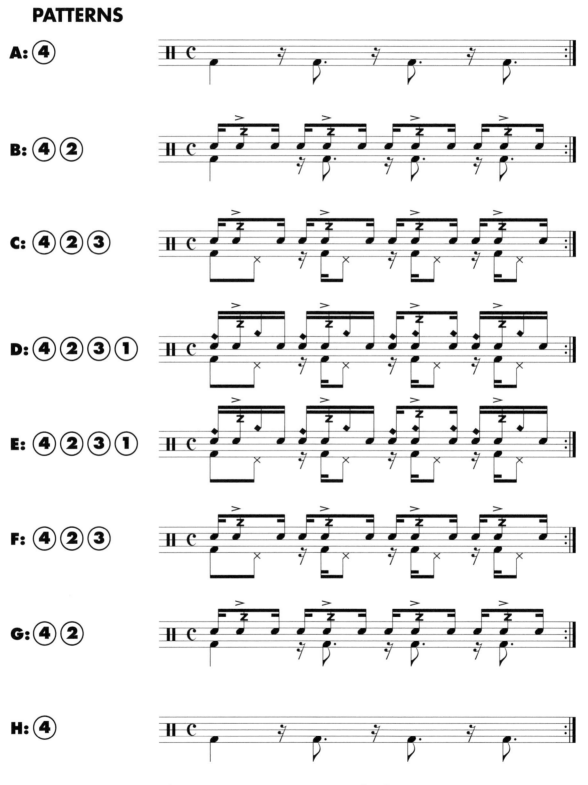

Try to create your own sequence for this exercise.

TRACK 15

MARACATU OSTINATO

Play the bass drum patterns over the following maracatu ostinato:

Bass Drum Patterns

Maracatu baque virado pattern

PRACTICE PROCEDURE

Play exercises 1 through 4 nonstop, repeating two times each.

GROOVES

The following grooves have elements of maracatu.

Funk/Pop With Maracatu Bass Drum

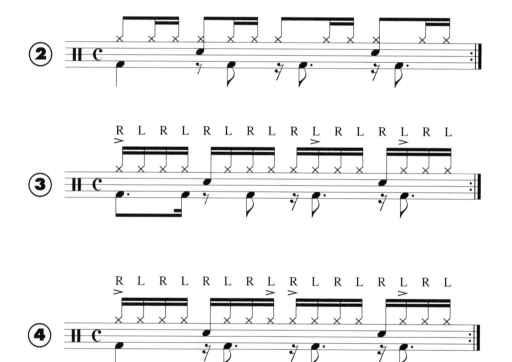

Maracatu Chart

"Maracafunk"

Christiano Galvão/João Gaspar

CHAPTER 3

FREVO
Hand Technique

Frevo is a Brazilian rhythm that is a great hand workout. In the following exercises you will have a chance to practice various aspects of hand technique such as speed, endurance, accents, and rolls—all at the same time. The example below is a basic frevo groove.

TRACK 20

FREVO

TRACK 21

EXERCISE #1: ROLLS

Play frevo with hand-to-hand sticking on the snare drum using the following rolls:
Start with tempo ♩ = 90

① Open Roll

R L R L R L R L   R L R L R R L L R R L L

② Buzz Roll

R L R L R L R L   R L R L R... L... R... L...

③ Six Stroke Roll
This example is used by the great frevo drummer Adelson Silva.

R L R L R L R L   R L R L R L L R R L

PRACTICE PROCEDURE

Play exercises 1, 2, and 3 nonstop repeating four times each. Use these metronome markings:

Ⓐ ♩ = 120

Ⓑ ♩ = 160

EXERCISE #2: ACCENTS

Use the frevo accents as drum phrases on the drumset. Practice slow to fast.

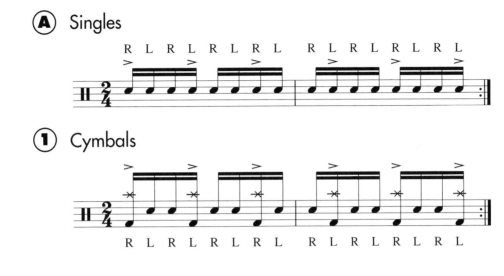

Ⓐ Singles

① Cymbals

STICKING WORKOUT

Play the frevo accents using right-hand-lead sticking. Accented notes: single; Unaccented: doubles. Repeat the exercise leading with the left hand. Try also to play the exercise as a four-bar phrase leading with both hands.

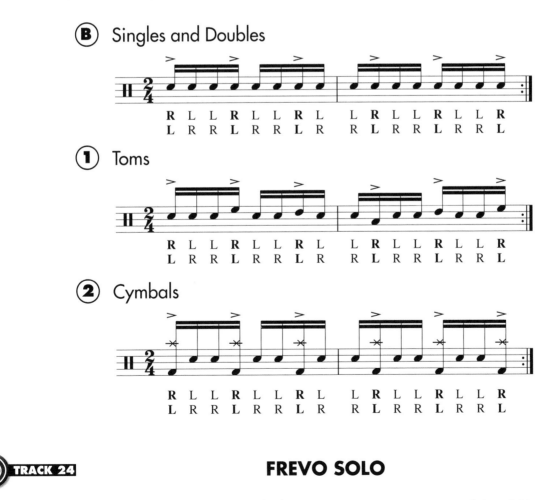

Ⓑ Singles and Doubles

① Toms

② Cymbals

FREVO SOLO

Make a frevo drum solo trying to apply the previous exercises: accents and the sticking workout.

GROOVES

The following grooves are some ideas of how to apply the frevo accents.

by Cesinha

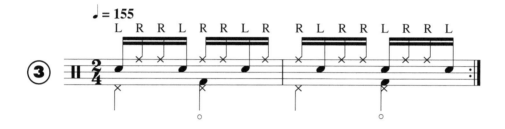

This page has been left blank to facilitate page turns for chart reading practice.

Frevo Chart

"Rain in Recife"

Alexandre Cavallo/Christiano Galvão

CHAPTER 4
SAMBA
Mixing Styles

Create interesting grooves mixing the rhythm of samba with elements of other styles.

 TRACK 29

SAMBA

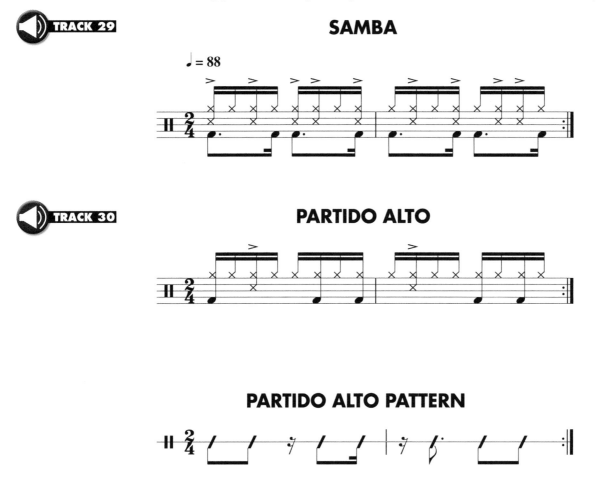

TRACK 30

PARTIDO ALTO

PARTIDO ALTO PATTERN

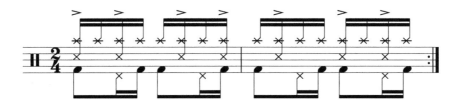 TRACK 31

SAMBA + PARTIDO ALTO

Play a partido alto crosstick pattern in a samba groove. This pattern is by Duduka da Fonseca.

SAMBA CRUZADO (CROSSED SAMBA)

Play a regular samba groove using the right hand on the snare drum while the left hand plays on the medium tom and the floor tom.

SAMBA CRUZADO EXERCISE

Play a samba groove using the right hand without accents on the snare drum. Play it softly.

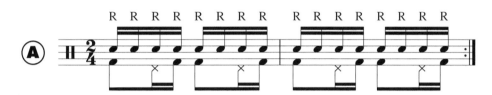

PARTIDO ALTO PATTERN

Play the partido alto pattern with the left hand on the floor tom and medium tom.

SAMBA CRUZADO + PARTIDO ALTO

Put examples A and B together to play samba cruzado with a partido alto pattern.

In this example by Duduka da Fonseca use the small and medium toms to expand the partido melody.

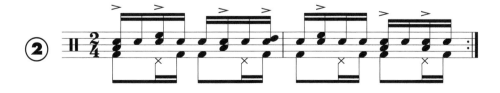

SAMBA + DRUM'N BASS (SAMBASS)

Mix the rhythm of samba with elements of the drum'n bass groove using the following subdivision:

GROOVES

Play a samba groove using the subdivision above to have the drum'n bass feel.

Hi-Hat

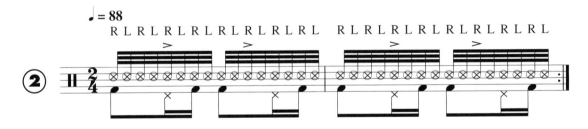

SAMBASS GROOVES

Snare w/ Brushes

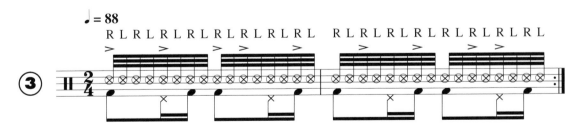

Snare w/brushes using samba accents

Drum'n Bass Chart

"Sambass"

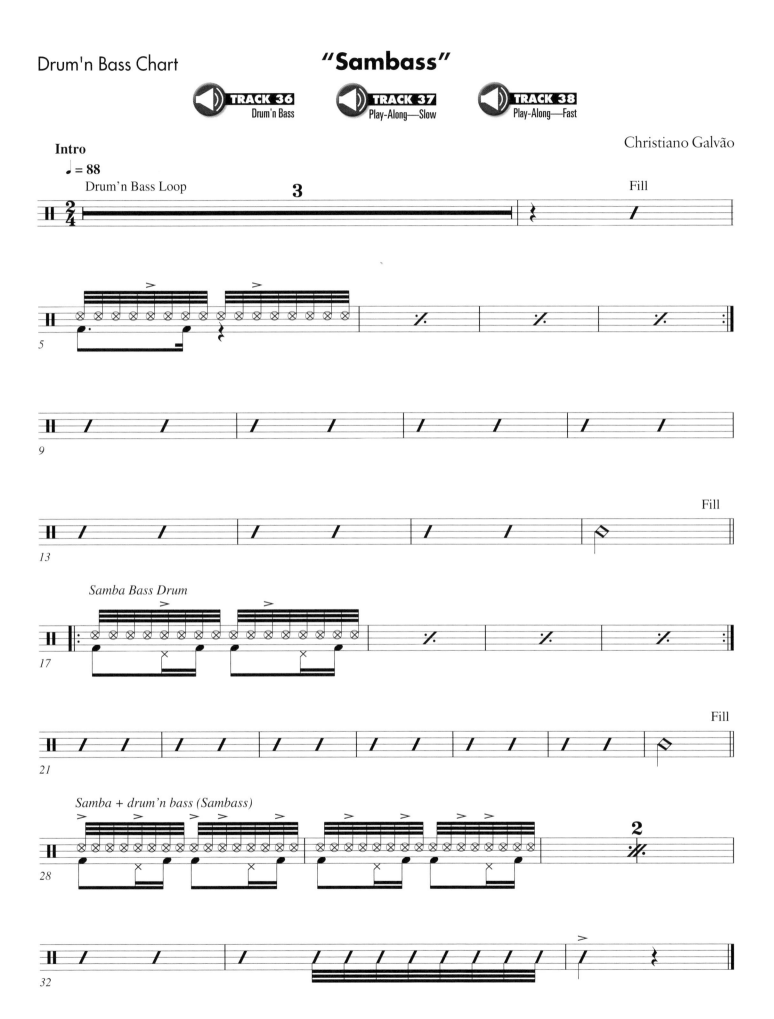

Christiano Galvão

Samba Chart

"Two Is Good, Three Is Samba"

Alexandre Cavallo/Christiano Galvão

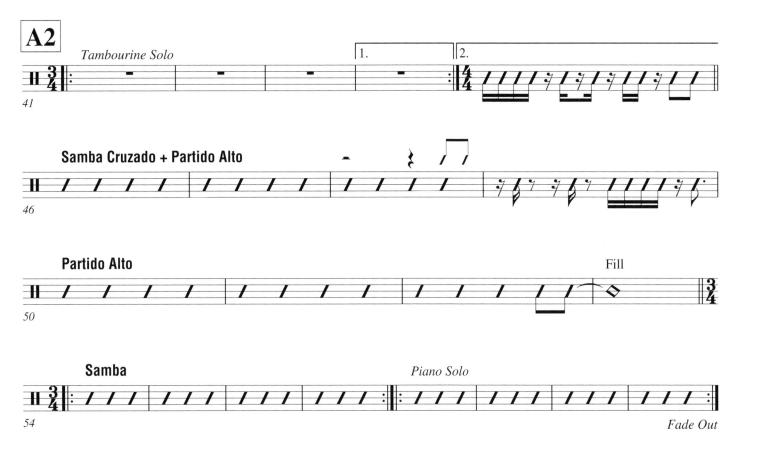

CREDITS

CD

Produced by Christiano Galvão
Recorded at Mamede's Studio - Rio de Janeiro/Brazil
Edited and mixed by Pedro Mamede
Songs mixed by Marcelo Sabóia at Musidisc Studio – RJ/Brazil
Mastered by Renato Luiz

SONGS

"Pumpkin with Coconut" / "Abóbora Com Coco" (Alexandre Cavallo/
    Christiano Galvão)
From CD *1+1* by Alexandre Cavallo and Christiano Galvão (2006)
Drums: Christiano Galvão
Bass: Alexandre Cavallo
Guitar: Fernando Caneca
Accordion: Chico Chagas

"Maracafunk" (Christiano Galvão/João Gaspar)
Drums: Christiano Galvão
Bass: Alexandre Cavallo
Guitars, Mandolin: João Gaspar

"Rain in Recife" / "Chuva no Recife" (Alexandre Cavallo/Christiano Galvão)
From CD *1+1* by Alexandre Cavallo and Christiano Galvão (2006)
Drums: Christiano Galvão
Bass: Alexandre Cavallo
Guitar: Fernando Caneca
Keyboard: Hirosh Mizutani
Percussion: Marcos Suzano

"Sambass" (Christiano Galvão)
Drums: Christiano Galvão
Synth Bass, Keyboard, Samples, Programming: Christiano Galvão

"Two Is Good, Three Is Samba" / "Dois é Bom, Três é Samba" (Alexandre
    Cavallo/Christiano Galvão)
From CD *1+1* by Alexandre Cavallo and Christiano Galvão (2006)
Drums and Brazilian Tambourine (Intro): Christiano Galvão
Bass: Alexandre Cavallo
Piano: Hamleto Stamato
Brazilian Tambourine and Percussion: Marcos Suzano

NOTES AND REFERENCES

IPC—Cassio Cunha/Multifoco Publishing
Modern Drummer magazine, July 1994. Duduka da Fonseca
Toque Junto—Renato Massa/Lumiar Publishing
Bateria Brasileira—Christiano Rocha
Acentos Ritmicos Brasileiros—Cassio Cunha/Multifoco Publishing
Prática de Bateria—Zequinha Galvão/Lumiar Publishing
Batuque é um privilégio—Oscar Bolão/Lumiar Publishing
The Language of Drumming DVD—Benny Greb/Hudson Music Publishing
Stick Control for the Snare Drummer—George Lawrence Stone/Alfred Publishing
Brazilian Rhythms for Drumset—Duduka da Fonseca and Bob Weiner/Manhattan
    Music Publishing

SPECIAL THANKS TO

Marco Socolli
Joe Testa and Ben Davis at Vic Firth Sticks
Kirsten Mat at Zildjian Cymbals
Northon Vanalli at Gretsch Drums (Sonotec)
Priscila and Simone Storino at Izzo Musical
Marcelo Juliani and Janeide at Pride Music
Jeff Schroedl, Jackie Muth and Nancy Ubick at Hal Leonard
Gustavo Faleiro, Pedro Mamede, Marcelo Sabóia, Renato Luiz and Paulo Marconi
Cassio Cunha and Elisa Crystal

RECOMMENDED LISTENING

SAMBA

Milton Banana Trio; drummer: Milton Banana.
Rosa Passos (any record).
Hamleto Stamato Trio (*Speed Samba Jazz*); drummer: Erivelton Silva.
Djavan (old records); drummer: Paulo "Briga" Vieira.
Hamilton de Holanda Quintet; drummer: Márcio Bahia.
Tom Jobim (any record).
Zeca Pagodinho (*MTV Live*); drummer: Jorge Gomes
Maria Rita (*Samba Meu Live*); drummer: Camilo Mariano

RECOMMENDED SAMBA DRUMMERS

Edison Machado, Mamão(Azimuth), Paulo Braga (Elis Regina/Tom Jobim), Robertinho Silva (Milton Nascimento), Wilson das Neves (Chico Buarque), Jorge "samba" Gomes (recording sessions), Pascoal Meirelles, Edu Ribeiro, Celso de Almeida, Camilo Mariano, Duduka da Fonseca, Kiko Freitas (João Bosco), Rafael Barata (Eliane Elias), Adriano de Oliveira (Leny Andrade), Teo Lima (Djavan/Ivan Lins).

BAIÃO

Luiz Gonzaga (all records).
Hermeto Pascoal (any record); drummers: Márcio Bahia and Nenê.
Egberto Gismonti (any record).
Gilberto Gil (Eu tu Eles)

MARACATU

Maracatu Nação Pernambuco (any record).
Lenine (any record); drummer: Pantico Rocha.
Nação Zumbi (*Afrociberdelia*).

RECOMMENDED MARACATU DRUMMERS

Cassio Cunha (Alceu Valença, Duna Project), Pupilo (Nação Zumbi).

FREVO

Spok Frevo Osquestra (any record) - Drummers: Adelson Silva and Augusto Silva.
Capipa (any record).
Duda do Frevo (any record).